Water...the Amazing Journey

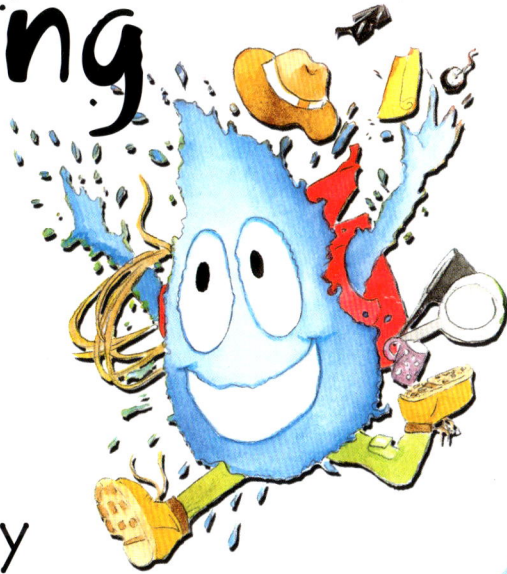

Written by

Caren Trafford

Illustrations by

Megan Eriksson

To be or not to be?

No water?...no question...

Anon

'When I grow up I want to be a camel.'

Water Droplet

Grade 1

Posters, Fact Sheets & Colouring Books available through
www.planetkids.biz

Published by Etram Pty Ltd
www.planetkids.biz

First published in
Australia 2004
3rd edition 2007

National Library of Australia
Cataloging-in-Publisher entry:
Trafford, Caren
Water...the Amazing Journey
ISBN 0-9581878-1-9

Illustrator: Megan Eriksson
Design: Flat Rabbits
Printed in China through
Bookbuilders

Aaah...Water!

What a great thing to have around. You can drink it, splash in it, swim in it, grow things with it and sometimes even skate on it, but have you ever sat down and had a really good chat with it?

Meet Wasu, a very wet, drippy, talkative water droplet. Wasu loves being a water droplet, after all who else travels everywhere for free, wears no clothes and never gets thirsty?

It is very normal to have long discussions on whose turn it is to be in the fish bowl

Water - it covers more than 70% of our planet and is constantly on the move. It can travel thousands of kilometres underground, just to pop up in the middle of a hot, dry desert. It can pour down huge waterfalls, gush through steaming jungles and drench ancient rainforests. Like a comic book superhero, water can change from solid to liquid to gas and back again but have you ever wondered where it all comes from, where it goes and what it does along the way?

Wasu knows the answers and he's here to tell you about the most amazing journey of all – the Journey of Water....

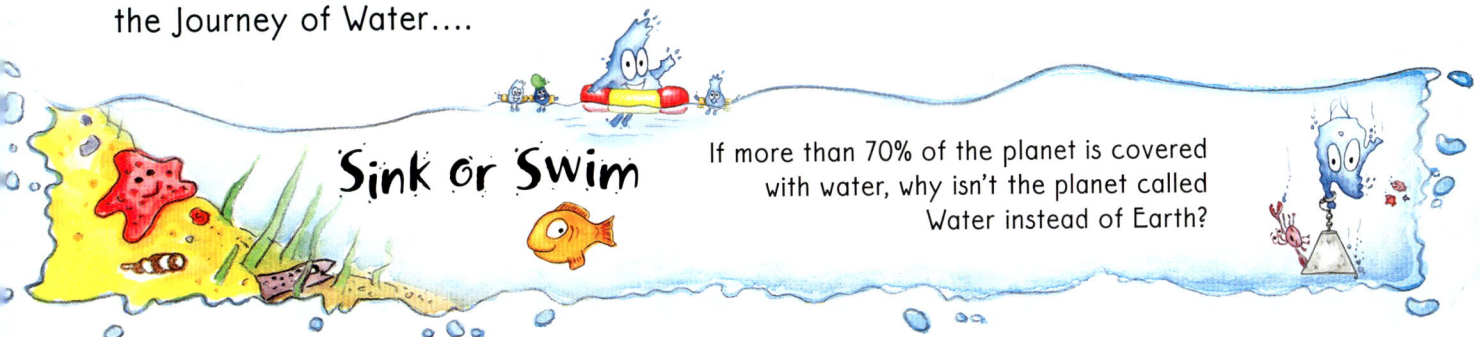

Sink or Swim

If more than 70% of the planet is covered with water, why isn't the planet called Water instead of Earth?

Who wants to be a water droplet?

Did you know that water has been around for almost as long as this amazing planet? In fact the water that you drank this morning could have been in the stomach of a giant dinosaur 65 million years ago.

Water may not look like much but it's the reason that our planet is so often called, 'The Blue Planet'. Without water, this planet would probably look like the Moon or even Mars.

However, there's far more to being a water droplet than just splashing around and making puddles. Without water, life as we know it would not exist. All life depends on it.

Water droplets have the most important job of all. Our job for billions of years has been to make sure that life can flourish. Wherever we travel we bring life. What a big responsibility!

So how do we do all this work? After all we are very small...

To get into Water Droplet School, you need to be a big drip

Sink or Swim If the earth was flat, the water covering the whole surface would be 3.7 km deep. It would take you about an hour and a half to walk that far but you would have to hold your breath...

2

In the beginning....

A very long time ago – well about 4.6 billion years ago - my ancestors, the ancient water droplets, got steamed up and swirled around in the gaseous atmosphere of this very hot, newly-formed planet.

Slowly, over billions of years, the planet cooled enough to allow us to condense and settle. Some of the more adventurous water droplets landed as ice packed comets. Others fell to the surface as rain, in the longest downpour imaginable. It was wet, very wet and umbrellas hadn't even been invented. As it rained, the water drained into great valleys, streams formed into rivers and slowly the seas and oceans began to fill.

Jumping out of things started longer ago than you would imagine

Do you have enough fingers and toes?

Earth contains an incredible amount of water. It's a little hard to count - but there are roughly 1,260,000,000,000,000,000,000 litres. According to some very clever people who can date rocks, the early seas formed around 3,800 million years ago. That's a lot of candles at my next birthday party!

Getting the right number of candles each year is quite a challenge

Sink or Swim

If there are 8.5 million litres of water available for each of the six billion people on this planet, why is it that one-third of the world's population does not have access to clean water?

3

When does 1+2 = ONE?

The secret of why water droplets are so cool is found in how we are made. Can you guess?

Water is made up of tiny bits called atoms. One larger atom of oxygen is linked to two smaller atoms of hydrogen. These three atoms are best buddies and hang out or bond together. Whenever they bond, they look just like the head of Mickey Mouse – but don't tell him that.

All these Mickey Mouse head look-alikes are water molecules and like to stick together. Humans describe this process as surface tension and it explains why water droplets keep their shape. We join up and hang out in oceans, lakes and puddles. Of course there are some exceptions, like crashing into a car windscreen when it rains... (then we run all over the place).

Being a water droplet is certainly never dull. Who's that calling us drips...?

Making water can create a big splash

Where does water like to chill out?

About 70% of the planet is covered by ocean. The average depth of the ocean is about 1,000 metres.

97% of the water on the planet is in the oceans and cannot be drunk because it contains salt.

90% of the planet's ice is in Antarctica.

About 2% of the planet's water is fresh, but 75% of that is in the polar ice caps and glaciers.

Another 0.36% is underground in aquifers and wells.

Only about 0.036% of the planet's total water supply is found in lakes and rivers. That's still thousands of trillions of litres, but it's only a tiny amount compared to all the water available.

The rest of the water is either floating in the air as clouds and water vapour, or is part of plants and animals.

Humans are 65% water and tomatoes are 95% water.

Who is your best friend?

One of the special things about water droplets is that we make a lot of friends. Did you know that some of our best mates are salty?

Around 3.5 billion years ago, salty water was the place to be. Do you know what a stromatolite is? It's a mound of bugs or microbes thought to be one of the first kinds of life and it grows happily in very salty sea-water. Back then, billions and billions of these critters hung out with our salty ancestors and became the first oxygen factories on our planet. Imagine…oxygen being created because of water's friendship with salt.

Pass the salt please….

Making new friends can be oceans of fun

You'd be surprised how often we meet up with someone we know

Sink or Swim

Why are the seas salty? As water flows through waterfalls, rivers and streams, it picks up small amounts of mineral salts from the rocks and soil in river beds and carries it all down to the sea. When the water in the seas and oceans evaporates or freezes, the salt is left behind.

5

What shall I wear?

Water is unique in many ways. Just look at us all; we hang around quite naturally in different states, solid, liquid or gas. We also behave differently when we get hot or cold. Most things expand when they are heated and shrink when they are cooled; we of course, do the exact opposite. As we freeze into ice, we get bigger and lighter which is why ice floats.

Another water-trick is to evaporate and disappear into thin air. We turn into a gas or vapour and waft around in clouds.

It can be quite a challenge changing from solid to liquid to gas and back again, especially when you are trying to decide what to wear in the mornings!

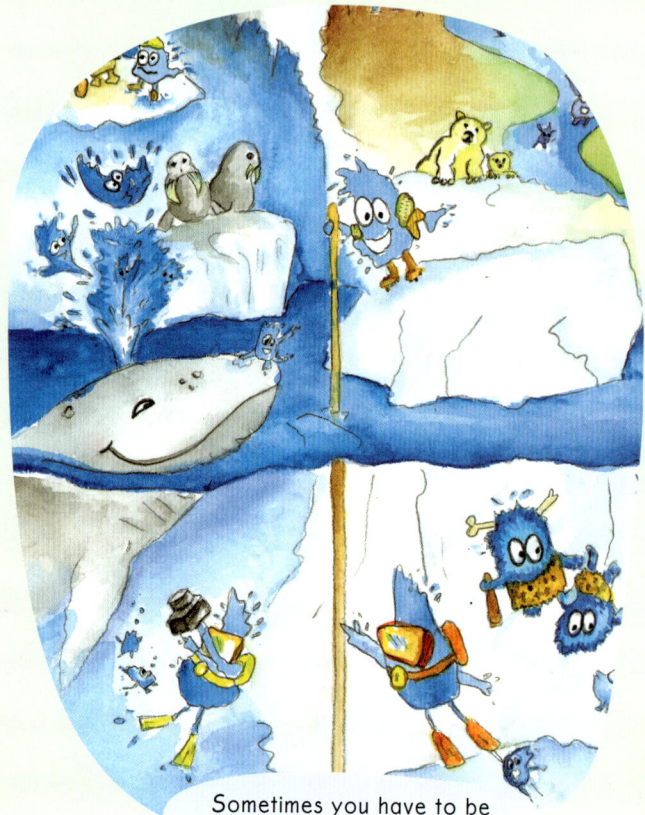

Sometimes you have to be brave and break the ice

Not knowing what state you will be in by the end of the day can cause some serious problems

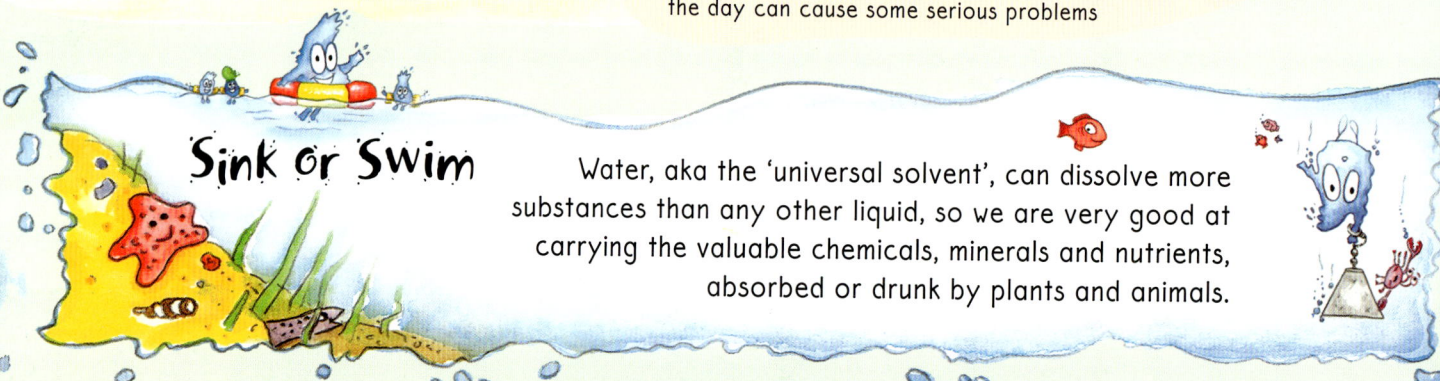

Sink or Swim

Water, aka the 'universal solvent', can dissolve more substances than any other liquid, so we are very good at carrying the valuable chemicals, minerals and nutrients, absorbed or drunk by plants and animals.

6

One way ticket to anywhere....

Water is always going somewhere. You don't believe me? Have you ever seen a stationary river?

For us, the most exciting part of river travel is floating along and whooshing down the waterfalls or wild waterslides we find along the way. Can you imagine surfing one of those incredibly white, foamy mountains of speed? It's awesome.

Waterfalls often become borders between different countries. We believe borders were invented to make it easier for humans to remember which language to speak, or which team to support. Fortunately water droplets don't worry about such things.

Great Waterfalls of the World

In Africa, Zambia and Zimbabwe are divided by Victoria Falls - considered to be the largest waterfall on the planet.

Niagara Falls is the second largest waterfall and acts as a border between Canada and the USA. 20% of all the surface fresh water in the world is in the four Upper Great Lakes and cascades over these falls.

Iguaçu Falls in South America, divides Argentina from Brazil. It came into existence after a huge volcanic eruption. Iguaçu means 'great water'.

Angel Falls has the longest (807 metres) single drop of any waterfall above ground. Located in Venezuela, it is named after a U.S pilot who crashed nearby while looking for gold.

The largest waterfall on Earth is actually underwater, in the Denmark Strait. It slowly cascades downward for 3.5 kilometres and is more than four times as tall as Angel Falls.

In some international competitions the players can be a little on edge

7

Can you go with the flow?

There is a huge network of watery places around the planet, all with different names.

Rivers are large natural streams of flowing water that empty into lakes, estuaries or oceans. Streams are smaller bodies of water that flow in natural channels and lagoons don't bother to go anywhere... they just collect.

The largest bodies of water are the oceans. Did you know that they are all connected to each other? Until the year 2000 there were only four oceans, but then a group called *The International Hydrographic Organisation* decided it was time for a new ocean. They named it the Southern Ocean – so now there are five oceans.

Seas are smaller parts of oceans, sometimes partly enclosed by land. All these different words may be confusing for you but for us, it's just a way to get around. We never need to get on a train, wait for a bus or even pump up the tyres on the bicycle... we just dive in and go with the flow.

Raging River Rides

The Amazon River is the widest river with the most flowing water. It accounts for 20% of all fresh water that drains from rivers into the oceans.

The Nile is the longest river in the world and one of the few to flow north. Egyptians have relied on the Nile flooding, for crop irrigation, for thousands of years.

The Missouri-Mississippi is the longest river system in North America. Mississippi means *'father of waters'* in the Algonquian Indian language.

The Yangzste River is the longest river in Asia. The world's biggest dam, the Three Gorges Dam, is on the Yangzste and provides Hydro Electric Power to the Chinese.

The Congo River in Africa is also known as the Zaire, meaning *'the mother of all rivers'*.

Sink or Swim
The Amazon River carries water through six countries from the Andes in Peru, through Bolivia, Venezuela, Colombia, Ecuador and Brazil, before emptying into the Atlantic Ocean.

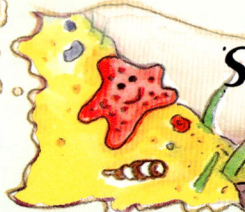

Sun-bathing beauties

At school, water droplets are always planning holidays. Our favourite class is MAJOR HOLS, or 'Many Amazing Journeys over Rivers, Highlands, Oceans, Lakes & Seas'. Humans however, just call our travels, the Water Cycle.

The Water Cycle is a technical term to explain our travel-plans. It shows how we seek out new lands and civilisations and move around the world.

To take part in the Water Cycle or MAJOR HOLS, water droplets must learn an important motto, *Be prepared.* Why? Well, you never know when we might be moved on to our next adventure. We could be snoozing on a leaf or paddling around in the dog's drinking bowl, when the sun or wind appear and lift us up, up and away. As we evaporate into the air, we change from a water droplet to a gas or vapour and drift around the sky. What a great view.

Later when the air cools, we often join up and form clouds. Depending on the temperatures, wind currents and land masses, we fall back to Earth as snow or rain and the Water Cycle continues.

More than 75% of all rain and snow falls into the sea. This constant recycling of water is critical to the health of the planet. Without it, much of the world would be barren and nothing would grow.

Not all water droplets are energetic and adventurous. The 'stay at home' types prefer to play with the fish and build sand castles at the bottom of the ocean. I only have one piece of advice for them. *If you want to stay home – DON'T go out sunbathing.*

Water students often have their heads stuck in the clouds

All water droplets know the importance of seat belts

Sink or Swim

The Pacific Ocean is the largest ocean in the world. It covers 28% of the planet's surface and is larger than all the dry land put together. It is home to the Mariana Trench where Challenger Deep, the deepest point on the planet lies, 10 kilometres beneath the surface. If Mount Everest was put in this trench, its peak would still be more than two kilometres below the surface!

On longer journeys many water droplets prefer a window seat

Water and the Weather

When water droplets get together in large bodies of water, like the seas and oceans, we can affect the weather and climate around the globe. Oceans store up huge quantities of solar energy as the water is heated by the sun. This heated water flows towards cooler waters, moving the heat away from the tropics, towards the icy regions at the North and South Poles. At the same time, a world-wide network of winds blows across the oceans, driving the currents and exchanging heat, moisture and gases with the water. This is how weather patterns are created. (By the way... currents are not things you make cakes with!)

Water spouts, thunderstorms, tidal waves, tsunamis, ...anyone want to tango...?

Waving to your dance partner at sea can create quite a storm

Ocean currents are the motorways of the planet. They transfer enormous quantities of water, nutrients and marine life from one place to another. The Gulf Stream pushes more water from the Gulf of Mexico and the Caribbean across the Atlantic into Northern Europe, than is carried by all the rivers on earth. The Gulf Stream is also a heating system for land lying in its path. Without this heating system, Norway would have the same freezing temperatures as Greenland which is often covered with thick sheets of ice. So, as you can see, water doesn't just cool things down, does it?

11

Natural passages...Extreme sports

Did you know that water droplets are the champions of extreme sport? You will find us in some of the most inaccessible places on the planet. We can boil and bubble away, in deep canyons towards the centre of the Earth, or settle as snow and ice, high up on mountain tops.

Pot Holing and Canyoning

Over millions of years, a great deal of fresh water has seeped down, through different layers of sedemimentary rock, below the Earth's surface. This water is called ground water. It can be millions of years old but like water droplets above ground, it is always on the move, flowing through geologic formations called aquifers. The Great Artesian Basin lies under 22% of Australia and is one of the largest aquifers in the world.

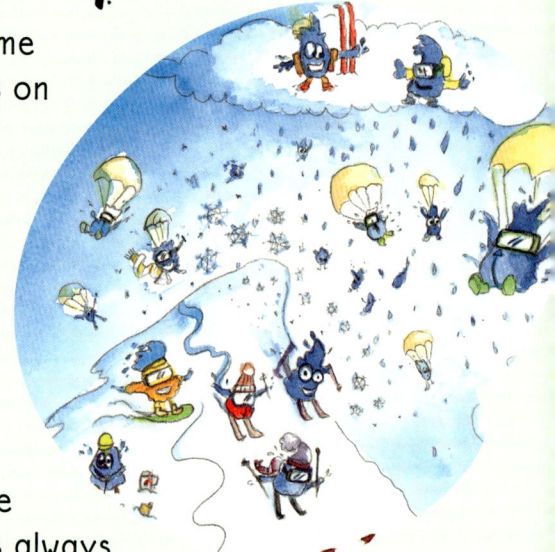

Bungee Jumping

Water also likes to get hot and steamy and rush up and out of the ground through geysers. Geysers start as underground volcanic springs. Magma or boiling hot rock heats the ground water, causing it to boil and steam. When it reaches a certain pressure it erupts and shoots into the air. *Wheee...*

Ice Caving

About 10% of the Earth's land area is covered with glaciers and ice sheets, some of which are millions of years old. Many of these moving masses of ice are found near the Poles, but they also exist on most of the world's continents, even Africa. Glaciers and ice sheets store about 75% of the world's fresh water so when you meet them, it's important to be nice.

Surf Boarding

'You can't make waves without wind.' This is an ancient saying among water droplets. Waves are created by the friction or the dragging motion of wind over the vast surface of the ocean. When big storms develop over oceans, fast winds create really big waves, sometimes called tidal waves, but they have nothing to do with tides! The biggest waves on the planet are called tsunamis (Japanese for 'harbour wave') and are caused by undersea earthquakes, volcanoes or landslides. It's the ultimate surf ride for a water droplet but not so good for anything or anyone that gets in the way.

Water is Life or is Life Water?

Looking for a new home? Why not consider water? Think of all the benefits. We have a great range of temperatures available and different amounts of oxygen, depending on whether you want to live near the surface or deep down in the abyss on the ocean's floor.

Some of your neighbours may become your food, others might try and eat you but nevertheless, we're a popular destination and we have some pretty famous residents already! For example, blue whales are the largest creatures on the planet and they live in the ocean. You can recognise them because their tongue weighs the same as an elephant.

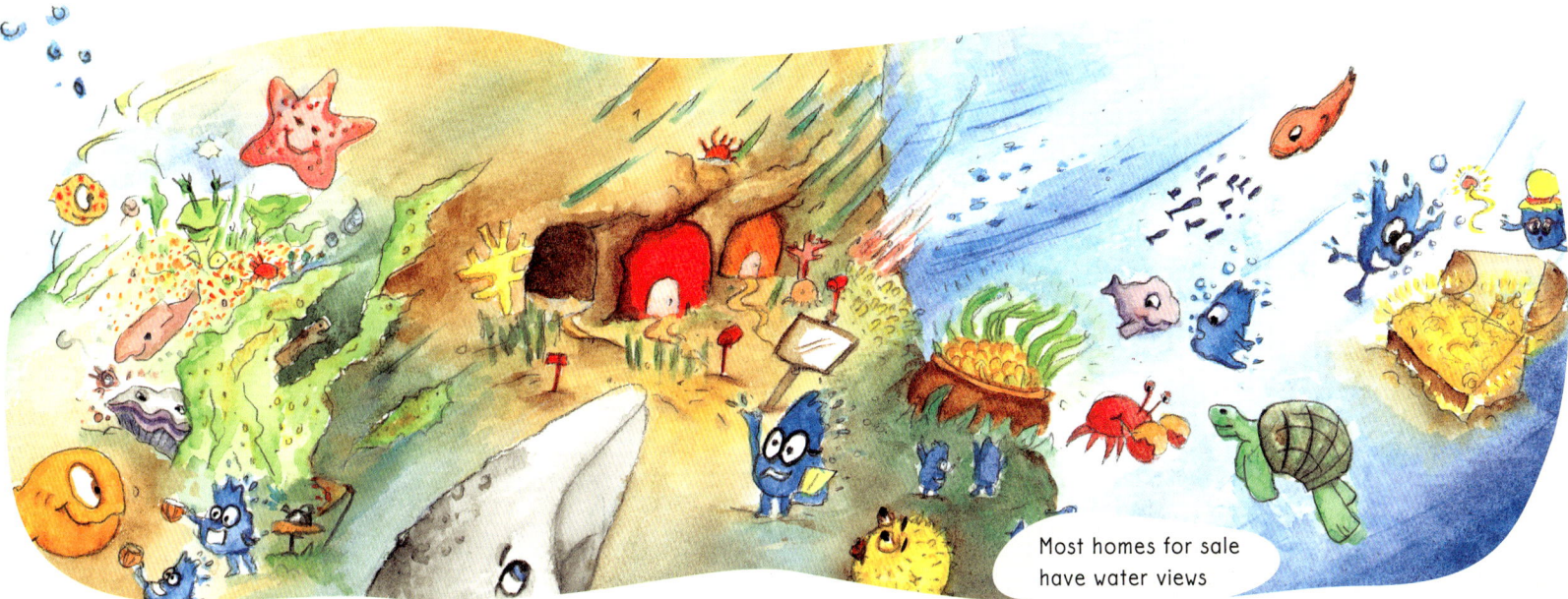

Most homes for sale have water views

Some of the smallest organisms also live in water. One cup of sea-water may not look like much but it can contain millions of bacteria, hundreds of thousands of phytoplankton and tens of thousands of zooplankton.

The Great Barrier Reef is the world's largest living structure and longest coral reef. Where is it? In the ocean. So, next time you are thinking of moving house, come and talk to us, we still have plenty of space available.

It is safe to say that wherever there is water, some form of life will want to move in.

Rainforest steaming

As well as providing food and housing for marine creatures, water droplets also spend many hours watering the land. In some parts of the world, we have so much fun pouring out of the sky that entire areas are named after us. Do you know what a rainforest is? It's a dense forest that grows in wet places with very heavy rainfalls.

Unfortunately, there aren't many rainforests left; nowadays they only cover 6-7% of the Earth, but they are believed to be home to nearly half the world's plant and animal species. So, whenever you visit a rainforest, take care and your camera.

Desert Life

Where do Humans Live?

Humans naturally prefer to live where there is water.

Two-thirds of the world's population - four billion people - live within 400 kilometres of a coast.

Just over half the world's population - around 3.2 billion people - occupy a coastal strip 200 kilometres wide, representing only 10% of Earth's land surface.

Africa, is the only continent where there are more people living in the interior, rather than along or near the coast.

Deserts on the other hand, are places where there is less than 25cm of rain a year. Here, we only make a small appearance, usually at an oasis where water rises to the surface from underground. Have you heard the saying, *'If the rain keeps up, there'll be a drought'*? That's how deserts come about. (No, that's not pudding.)

The Atacama Desert in Northern Chile is the driest desert in the world. Some parts of the Atacama have not seen rain for centuries. It is thought to be between 10 and 15 million years old, making it the oldest desert on Earth.

Sink Or Swim

Did you know that the driest and one of the wettest places in the world are next to each other? The mountains that collect all the rainfall to make the largest river in the world - the Amazon River - are also responsible for preventing the Atacama Desert, which is right next door, from receiving any rainfall.

Our Mission: To seek out new lands

I don't like to boast, but water is responsible for some of the world's greatest inventions and achievements! Without water, the ancient civilisations could not have flourished, philosophers would not have sat around in hot tubs discussing the meaning of life and the inventions of the industrial, modern and technological ages would not have been possible.

Irrigation means Civilisation

Many good ideas spring from water

What did all the early ancient civilisations have in common? You guessed it - WATER. Because humans do not find it so easy to go with the flow, they did not want to walk great distances to find fresh water and so they built their cities near the water.

As populations increased, a more regular supply of fresh water was needed and before long, ways to irrigate, or water the soil on a large scale, were invented.

The Egyptian civilisation developed more than 5,000 years ago. It was dependant on the annual flooding of the River Nile and massive irrigation works were built to control its flow. The Egyptians' world was defined by water and they believed that each day, the Sun God Ra sailed in a solar boat, across a sky made of water. Each year they looked to their Pharaoh, whom they believed to be their Gods' representative on Earth, to make the Nile flood, so crops could be planted in the rich silt carried by the flood waters. From a water droplet's point of view, this was a great way to see the Egyptian countryside. Water droplets would queue up for days just for the opportunity to irrigate the land and see the Great Pyramids.

Lots of new ideas were floated at this time

15

Early water carriers

Throughout the ages water has been drunk out of everything, from gold cups to dirty hands.

Did you know that the water you drink, bathe or swim in today, could be the same water that was carried along in the great Roman aqueducts of the ancient world and drunk by one of those Roman emperors, thousands of years ago?

Roman aqueducts were water-carrying systems that used gravity to carry water from the mountains, down through tunnels built in hillsides, to the towns and farms below. Roman water droplets thought this was great. It was the first time that we were 'on tap' and could visit cities on a flow-through basis.

Roman baths led to a huge increase in water demand...it just poured in...

The aqueducts allowed us to explore whole new areas previously 'off limits'. Even today, we can pop up as tourists in Rome, because the city's fountains are still supplied by water that comes from freshwater springs in the hills above the city.

It did not take long for humans to realise that water could also be used to transport people and goods across land. Waterways or canals were built as short-cuts between different regions. This was wonderful. Finally, we could boldly go to places where no water droplet had gone before!

The waterproof camera was invented for a very good reason

What's a Qanat?

While some ancient civilisations built aqueducts and canals, others dug for water. During the Roman era, the qanat system was introduced in Egypt and Syria. A qanat is a water supply system using underground water sources trapped in hillsides. Gravity pulls the water downhill through a series of tunnels, sometimes several kilometres long. Even today, much of the water in the plateau regions of Iran is below ground and is brought to the surface this way. There are hundreds of kilometres of qanats in Iran, Western China, Afghanistan, Libya, Algeria and Morocco. Qanats are cheaper than drilling wells for water and are used in many technology-poor areas.

Are there any bored water droplets?

In other parts of the world where surface water is limited, water from underground is often an alternative. Western Australia, for example, uses twice as much ground water as surface water. Even though the land above ground is dry, bores are drilled down and pumps and the pressure bring the water up to the surface. It can be quite a surprise when we pop up for a visit, that's for sure!

The good five star resorts get booked up months in advance

How to stay wet without getting your feet dry

Grand Canal
One of the greatest water constructions was the Grand Canal, built in China more than 2,000 years ago. When it was finished it was 1600 kilometres long and is still the world's longest man-made waterway.

Panama Canal
This is a short cut between the Atlantic and the Pacific Oceans. Built in seven years between 1907 and 1914, it is 80 kilometres long.

Suez Canal
Considered the busiest canal in the world, 14% of the world's ships pass through it. Connecting the Mediterranean Sea with the Indian Ocean, this is a short cut for ships which don't want to sail around the entire coast of Africa. Partially built by the Pharaohs around 300 BC, it was finally opened in 1869 and is 163 km long.

Venice Canals
In the end, humans got so carried away with their canals that they built an entire city around them. Venice, Italy, is linked by a series of more than 150 canals and 400 bridges. You either need to be a water droplet or have good shoes to get around.

17

See the sea or boat in a moat?

Humans can be quite smart. When they saw the great adventures water droplets have travelling around, they decided to copy us. So, they built themselves a wonderful selection of boats and ships.

Ships are one of the oldest and most important means of transportation, but do you know how they move? Humans think they float but let me tell you a secret...they are carried around by water droplets!

By the Middle Ages, water had another very important job – defense. We poured into the moats around many castles; acted as the first line of defence against attacking armies and were often boiled up in huge cauldrons and tipped out, onto the unfortunate soldiers below. We were so busy, we didn't know whether we were dripping or dropping.

Empires grew because their vast fleets of ships explored, conquered and took control of the trade routes. What exciting times! Pirates sailed the seven seas looking for loot and plunder; great sea battles were fought and huge amounts of treasure was sunk.

Today water is busier than ever. 90% of trade between countries is carried by ships and about half the telephones between nations are connected using giant underwater cables.

Castle life often flowed around in circles

Great assortments of ships constantly travel across the seas and oceans. There are tankers carrying oil and petrol; refrigerated ships taking fresh fruit, meat and vegetables and bulk carriers moving mountains of coal and grain. Cargo containers transport manufactured goods like cars and computers and some ships are more than three football fields long!

My favourite ships are the luxury passenger liners. I do have one question. Why are there swimming pools on deck, when the ship is surrounded by water?

Steam boats proved a huge distraction for water droplets

Water is Power

You may think that water droplets are wet drips but when we put our heads together, we create more power than you could imagine. We can carve channels so deep through rock, that you can see them from the moon. Have you ever seen the Grand Canyon? It is a huge chasm, hundreds of metres wide, carved through kilometres of rock and we created it!

It took humans a while to recognise the power of water but over the centuries, we have found ways of working together.

Because humans don't get around as often as we do, they like to sit down and invent things. Around 200 B.C, water wheels were invented. These were used to grind grain and irrigate crops, but did you know that water wheels are the ancestors of modern day Hydro Electric Power? (Hydro means water.) Today, Hydro Electric Power produces about 20% of the world's electricity. How does it

work? In the same way that water droplets get together and take rides in the cogs of a water wheel to make it turn, a bit like taking a ride on the Big Wheel at a fun fair, Hydro Electric Power is the result of huge numbers of water droplets, meeting up and turning enormous blades in turbines.

To make electricity, water needs to be stored in vast quantities, so a lake or reservoir is created by building a dam. Then, the gates within the dam are opened, allowing some of us to flow through a series of pipes that get smaller and smaller.

Everything was fine until Wasu, Aqua and Hydro tried to turn the water wheel the wrong way

Explaining the MAJOR HOLS to farmers is not always as easy at it might seem

As we squeeze ourselves through, we speed up and finally push against the blades of a turbine, which spins a generator and POW... electricity. Once our work is done, we are carried through more pipelines and rejoin the river downstream. What a relief to stretch our legs again – it's quite a squeeze, getting through those turbines.

Why do humans need electricity? Our *gurgle* search engine shows that it's used for lots of things...powering your cities, heating, keeping cool, light, refrigeration, computers and much more. I told you that we worked well together.

Water droplets are fountains of knowledge in many fields

Hydro Electric Power may be a great way to produce clean electricity, but it can also create many problems. Building a dam can flood huge areas and change the natural water flow of the river. Farmers, fishermen and anyone who uses the river for transport, food or water will be affected and sometimes many thousands of people need to be moved. It's not just people that are affected. When a river is dammed, the living conditions in the river below the dam also change. There is less water which means fewer currents, less oxygen and less life. Ecosystems downstream suffer badly and the impact on the environment can be tremendous. So, the next time you are thinking of building a dam, please make sure you consider all the consequences and alternatives...

Natural Dam Builders

Beavers are well known for their engineering skills. They have strong front teeth, making it easy for them to gnaw through trees and they can build dams without the use of concrete or cement. These dams create ponds and wetland ecosystems. Why do they build dams? Perhaps it's because the sound of rushing water annoys them and they prefer peace and quiet.

20

Have you ever met an unfit water droplet?

Humans are made up of 65% water and many of the body's organs are mostly water. In order to stay healthy, it is really important for you to drink fresh water. We don't mind one bit because after all, what goes in, must come out.....

Your body is like a giant chemical factory and water is essential for many of the chemical reactions that make it work. We help to regulate body temperature, carry nutrients from the digestive system around your body and move out the waste. If you don't drink water your body will dry out; you become dehydrated and feel unwell. In fact, if you stopped drinking water for any length of time you would become very sick and even die!

Water droplets need to stay healthy and so do you, so drink fresh, clean water ...we're very good for you.

Damming Dam Building

In the 1930s, the construction of huge dams that blocked entire river basins began. In 1936, the Hoover Dam (US) was completed. It is visible from space.

The Itaipu Dam is a 7.7 kilometre complex of dams at the Brazil-Paraguay border. It has 18 generators, took 18 years to build and cost US$18 billion. Before building it, engineers had to change the course of the Parana River, the seventh largest river in the world.

The biggest hydro power plant and concrete dam in the world will be the Three Gorges Power Plant, in China. It will generate 12% of China's power. When completed in 2009, it will stretch more than 1.5 kilometres across the Yangtze River. More than one million people will be displaced. The 560 kilometre reservoir will submerge villages, ancient temples, burial grounds and canyons.

World-wide, 19% of the world's electricity generation comes from dams. Dams also provide the irrigation for almost 16% of the world's food.

About 80 million people have been displaced by dam construction and the loss of ecosystems, wildlife, forests and biodiversity cannot be measured. Do you dam the dam? The balance is never easy....

Water doesn't grow in taps

Those who live in a city know how easy it is to open the tap and watch fresh, clean water flow out. But as you now know, water doesn't grow in taps and many people do not have taps for fresh water. In some places, people must collect water from several kilometres away and carry it home, in buckets. Many villages rely on communal canals, while other people must draw water by hand, from wells dug into the ground.

There are about six billion people in the world today. Almost half of them live in towns and urban areas and are lucky enough to have water on tap, or to be more precise, out of a tap. In these areas, huge systems of pipes, dams and water treatment plants have been built, to ensure a constant, clean supply of water. Isn't that wonderful?

It's good to travel light – you never know where you might drop in

Humans providing homes for water droplets. Large areas of land called 'water catchments', are set aside to catch the rain, run-off and surface water, all of which is pumped to a water filtration plant.

At the filtration plant we pass through large sieves to remove twigs, weeds and any fish. Next, tiny particles of dirt are removed. In some places, fluoride is added to help protect your teeth and chlorine is added to clean the water and kill off any nasty bugs. It's nice to be cleaned up sometimes, a bit like visiting a beauty parlour before the big night out.

Then, all spruced up, we are pumped through pipes to large water storage reservoirs where we are held until needed. When it's our turn, we flow through a series of pipes and pumping stations to your home, ready for you to turn on the tap. *Whoosh!* Time for a cup of tea.

Beauty parlours are a great place to relax before a big date

Water doesn't hang out at your house for very long, but it's nice to visit. After having a good look around, we can be flushed down the toilet, float down the plug hole or drained down the sink – it's all slippery slides to us.

Water droplets love to flow down holes and when we leave your house, we travel through a different set of pipes which usually flow down to the sewer system. Next, we make our way to the Wastewater Treatment Plant. Here, humans very kindly tidy us up again and separate us from the sludge and other bits and pieces that also find their way down these pipes. Then, we are ready to be sent back into the environment, on our travels again, (without even a packed lunch, I might add).

When you wave goodbye to us, as we gurgle down the plug hole, don't think that we are all waste! Before we leave your area, we'd be very happy to be recycled. Water from your hand-basins, washing machines, showers and baths can easily be reused in the garden or for landscape irrigation. This recycled water is called *grey water* and used with care, it is brilliant for watering your gardens.

Water is described in many colours...blue, green, brown, turquoise, aquamarine... but what colour is recycled water?

Going around the bend happens every day

23

Water water everywhere... but not enough to drink

World-wide there is plenty of water, enough for everyone. However, because water is pretty independent and not evenly distributed, we do not always fall, or turn up, at the right time and in the right place. If we did, there wouldn't be so many droughts and water shortages in one part of the world, at the same time as huge floods in another.

Many countries rely on seasonal rains for their fresh water supply. India, for example, can have a whole year's rainfall in a couple of weeks.

Unfortunately these rains often take the form of monsoons which can cause surging floodwaters and are impossible to collect, so water remains scarce. At the other extreme, some countries like Australia and parts of Africa, suffer from years of drought.

It's hard to believe but two-thirds of the world's population - around four billion people - live in areas which only receive one-quarter of the world's annual rainfall.

24

Even air traffic controllers cannot always get us to land in the right place

WWWW = World-Wide Water Wastage

Why is so much water wasted? Just look at these facts reported by water droplets around the world.

Sinking while drinking.

The world's largest metropolis, Mexico City, is sinking because of the amount of water being pumped out from under its foundations. Bangkok and Venice are two more cities sinking because their ground water is not being managed properly.

Is oil more precious than water?

One of the largest freshwater wetlands is in Southern Sudan. It is being drained in the search for oil. How much water do you think is being wasted by doing this?

Would you drink what goes down the sink?

Many cities in the developing world are polluting their own water supplies because their wastewater is seeping back into the same ground which holds their fresh water supply.

Use it too much and you'll lose it.

China's Yellow River is so over-used that for an average of 70 days a year, over the past 10 years, its waters have dried up.

Spray away?

Traditional farming techniques add to water wastage. In Europe if these practices continue, more than 40% of all groundwater reserves will be polluted with fertilisers and pesticides by 2025.

Swim in the sewer?

Raw sewage is still being pumped into some of the world's oceans. Lima, in Peru, discharges 18,000 litres of wastewater per second into the Pacific Ocean.

Going...going...

In agriculture, about 60% of water seeps from distribution channels and is lost. Using current farming methods, it takes three cubic metres of water to produce one kilo of rice and 1000 tonnes of water to produce one tonne of grain.

How much will it cost?

Countries which are short of water are already buying it. Jordan imports 91% from abroad, Israel 7%, Saudi Arabia 50% and Egypt 40%.

Where will the next drop come from?

By 2025, the world will need to make available 20% more water to supply the extra three billion people expected on the planet. By then, one in every three people – mostly in developing countries – will struggle to find water.

Leaky pipes?

The proportion of households in major cities connected to piped water is 100% in North America, compared with only 43% in Africa. In some places, leaky pipes lose as much as 40% water.

Watch where you chuck your muck...

Water droplets see a lot of very dirty business. Even where there is plenty of fresh water, people, industry and agriculture still manage to make it dirty by pouring their rubbish into it. Isn't that a strange place to put your muck if you want a drink?

There is an estimated 12,000 km of polluted water worldwide - more than the total amount of water contained in the world's ten largest river basins. What a lot of muck floating around the place...*phew!* It takes eight litres of clean water to clean one litre of dirty water. As concerned water droplets who want to make water count, this seems an awful waste.

Water pollution affects more than just humans. It also destroys the freshwater ecosystems that are home to great numbers of animals, birds, fish and all those tiny critters you can't even see.

Because of pollution, 20% of freshwater fish are threatened, endangered, or have become extinct.

Water droplets everywhere are very troubled with these reports. To make matters worse, the demand for fresh, clean water is increasing. Over the last 100 years, it has risen by 700%.

By our calculations, water around the world is not only being used, it is being used UP! Water mismanagement, wastage, pollution, industry overuse and the continuing increase in the world's population are all using up the fresh supplies of water.

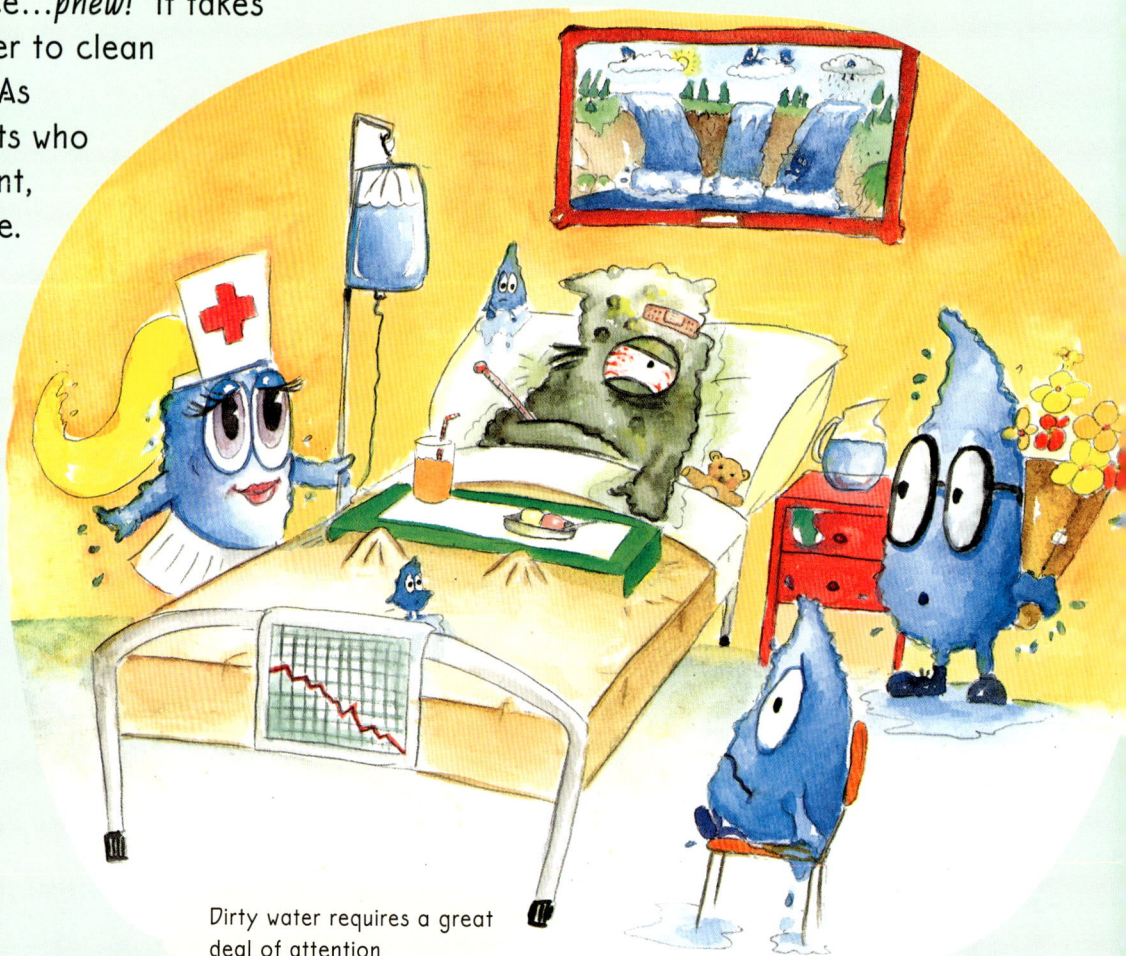

Dirty water requires a great deal of attention

Time to come clean

Water droplets everywhere are asking for your help. Although some humans realise that water is the most precious drop and are trying to conserve us, everyone needs to be involved. There are so many ways to look after water droplets. You may think that we like to be pampered, taken to the movies or bought dinner. Of course we do, but most of all, we like it when humans treat us properly and value us.

We've seen some improvements in recent times but there's still a long way to go. Can you think of ways to save water? Here are just a few...

Farm smart

Because 70% of the world's available fresh water is used for irrigation, any improvement in crop planting, watering and harvesting will have a big effect on the fresh water supply. More efficient use of water, such as drip irrigation, where the watering system is applied to the roots of suitable plants and crops, is one easy way to save water and still get bumper crops. It works at home in the garden too.

Look after Natural Areas

Monitoring and cleaning up polluted rivers and stopping the destruction of forests and wetland regions, will help conserve water catchments and will provide more clean water for the millions of people that have barely a cup of water per day. Nature's wetlands clean water naturally. In the last 100 years, over 50% of the world's wetlands have been lost. 300-400 million people live near wetlands. If you look after these special ecosystems, they will clean us up for you to enjoy and it won't cost a thing.

Water in the Bank

It is even possible to put water back into the ground. Some water companies have discovered how to store water when they have a surplus and re-use it in times of drought. Thames Water in the United Kingdom has created an artificial recharge scheme. A giant aquifer acts as a gigantic sponge which stores extra water when it is available. We love this – a new holiday destination, underground.

27

Dollars or Drops

OK - how much would you pay for a clean glass of water? What about if you were really thirsty? How much should factories and farmers pay for water? What is the true cost of using rivers as rubbish dumps? If people were charged a realistic amount to use water, would they be more careful with it? In drought-prone areas, water is being rationed and fines are imposed on those who squander water or use it unwisely. Industry is beginning to be made to pay the true price of using water, instead of just having us as a free resource. It's a start but can you help as well?

The water police are always on the look-out for drips

Do it yourself

If every house was built with a rainwater tank, think how much water you could collect. If you recycled your water, how much could you save? In some parts of the world where there are seasonal rains, people build dams underground to collect water during the rainy season. That way they'll have plenty of water during the dry spells.

How does Water Count?

Many kids are learning that water counts. Some of the clever, water wise ones are even teaching others. In your home, turning off dripping taps and fixing leaky pipes are huge water savers. Recycling water is another great idea – we love being invited back to your place for another visit.

Does your house have a water-saving tap? Do you take big baths or short showers? Do you turn off the tap when you brush your teeth? Do you have a rainwater tank? When you grow up, will you help to save the wetlands or invent new techniques to help farmers use water more wisely when they grow their crops? Will you discover a way to help industry use less water or a power source that does not rely on water?

28

All invitations gladly accepted

May the Source be with you

Fortunately there are some clever humans who are learning how to be water wise. We hope to hear from all adventurous water droplets travelling around the planet, that more and more humans are using us with care and understanding that water is the most precious drop.

There is enough water for everyone, if you treat us right. After all, we don't eat much and are quite easy to watch out for. We love being part of life – it's so exciting and we don't want to run out on you. So, let's make a deal! Look after us and we will be able to look after you and all living things, as we continue our amazing journey, around this wonderful blue planet.

P.S Next time you see us...don't forget to wave.

29

Spouts and Slides... the

Help Wasu and his friends save the world's water supply. Trave wise so that there is enough fresh, clean water for everyone. slides on an amazing journey to the Source and the prize. Are

Spouts Legend

1C	Master the Cycle and fast track through Water Droplet School
1F	De-bug watering system to make grey water safe for gardens
1H	Smart farmers put in drips
1K	Bright drop genius invents machine to power cars with water
2C	Super-wet water drip invents teleport system to replace cars
3A	Desert oasis saves lost travellers
3H	Discover meditation and learn to become the water not the salt
4F	Solar power means huge dams are no longer necessary
4K	Plug pulled on rubbish dumped in rivers
4L	Water-wise kids teach parents how to save water
5C	Judges declare water to be the most precious drop
6B	Rainwater tank rebates increased by government
6F	Old geysers used as alternate power
7F	Major cities stop pumping raw sewage into oceans
7G	Desalination plant turns salty seawater into fresh drinking water
7J	Trickle of rainwater tanks installed becomes a flood
7K	Let off steam in bathroom with shorter shower

A B C D E F

8 7 6 5 4 3 2

START A B C D E F

Quest for the Source

around the world making sure that water counts. Let's be water-
Follow Wasu and friends up the Spouts and down the Water-
you ready? Just get some counters & throw a dice to begin…

G H I J K L

8
7
6
5
4
3
2
1

G H I J K L

Slides Legend

2E	Tap left running while cleaning teeth
2J	Water wasters caught wet handed
3E	Tanker oil spill kills inland sea
3J	Mad scientist thaws Pole and floods planet
4B	Water thieves escape with precious water droplets
4J	Leaky pipes lose large amount of fresh water supply
6E	Pollution from local industry kills more wetlands
6H	Get bottled on supermarket shelf
6I	Judge sentences sorcerer's apprentice for wasting water
7A	Freshwater fish protest for better living conditions
7L	Sucked down into the abyss and get sat on by creature from the deep
8C	Water police catch gang sending rubbish down river
8E	Rain keeps up causing major drought
8I	Meet thirsty dinosaur and miss birthday party

Why do water droplets wear wellies?

To keep their feet wet!

What travels everywhere for FREE, wears no clothes and never gets thirsty?

Water – it covers 70% of our planet and is always on the move. Meet Wasu, our favourite water droplet and discover water's view on life. Follow the Water Cycle, travel through the ages and discover things you never knew. Why is water so important? Where does it go? What does it do in its spare time?

In today's climate of drought, water conservation needs everyone to take part. Let's find out how we can help Wasu and the water droplets manage water so there is enough for future generations. Read the book; enjoy the journey and may the Source be with you.

'If you thought you knew water, then think again. This book guarantees to give you a fun and innovative look at our planet's most plentiful resource. It will immerse you in a sea of facts that you never knew existed!'
Jon Dee,
Founder of Planet Ark

'Utterly charming, witty, informative, well-paced, and just well...gushing humour and a nice strong message of concern for the environment.. an exquisite FOUNTAIN of knowledge.'
Margaret Gee,
Literary Agent & Author

'It's not PLANET EARTH, surely? It should be PLANET WATER. Caren has done it again! The most pellucid, penetrating and panoramic paeon to H$_2$O I've ever seen. A sopping great triumph…It's brilliant.'
Robyn Williams, AM,
Presenter,
ABC Science Show

'Once again an amazing, entertaining and informative blend of humour, story and science.'
Mike Lotzof,
CEO, Australian Compliance Institute

'A wonderful book which raises some thought provoking questions as it explores the importance of one of our most precious resources.'
Fiona Robertson,
Environmental Scientist

Always on the look out for interesting interviews, this time Caren Trafford has managed to corner Wasu, a very talkative water droplet. Although you might wonder which planet she comes from, she actually lives in Sydney with her boys, Oscar and Kody and her husband, Mike.

ISBN 0-9581878-1-9
9 780958 187817

HOW TO LAUNCH A TECH START-UP

ROBOTICS, GAMING AND OTHER TECH JOBS

For Acer
M.Y.

To the brilliant, imaginative and
responsible minds behind technology.
S.L.

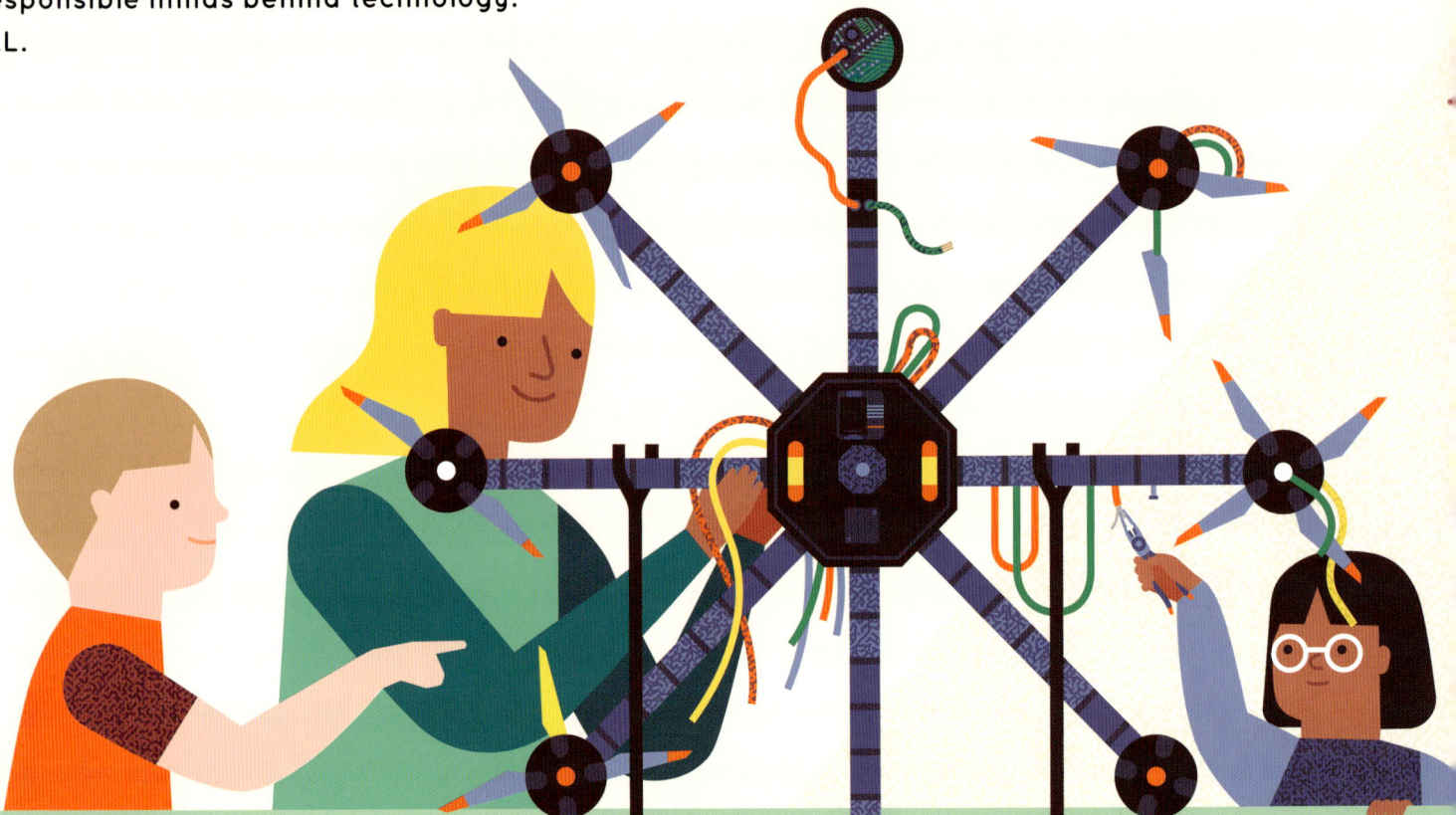

First published 2024 by Nosy Crow Ltd
Wheat Wharf, 27a Shad Thames, London, SE1 2XZ, UK

Nosy Crow Eireann Ltd
44 Orchard Grove, Kenmare, Co Kerry, V93 FY22, Ireland

www.nosycrow.com

ISBN 978 1 83994 954 8 (HB)
ISBN 978 1 83994 953 1 (PB)

Nosy Crow and associated logos are trademarks
and/or registered trademarks of Nosy Crow Ltd

Text © Michelle You 2024
Illustrations © Sol Linero 2024

The right of Michelle You to be identified as the author
and Sol Linero to be identified as the illustrator of this work
has been asserted.

A CIP catalogue record for this book is available from the British Library.

Printed in China following rigorous ethical sourcing standards.

Papers used by Nosy Crow are made from wood grown in sustainable forests.

10 9 8 7 6 5 4 3 2 1 (HB)
10 9 8 7 6 5 4 3 2 1 (PB)